Gym Business

The Success Formula for Maximizing Revenue and Member Retention

Ghazwan Alemara

Copyright © 2024 Ghazwan Alemara. All rights reserved.

No part of this publication may be reproduced, distributed, or transmitted in any form or by any means, including photocopying, recording, or other electronic or mechanical methods, without the prior written permission of the publisher, except in the case of brief quotations embodied in critical reviews and certain other noncommercial uses permitted by copyright law.

For permissions requests or inquiries, please contact the publisher at hello@ghazwanalemara.com

Published by ghazwanalemara.com

Contents

Contents 3
Introduction 1
Understanding the Gym Business Landscape 4
    The Evolution of the Fitness Industry 4
    Identifying Key Revenue Streams 8
    The Role of Member Retention in Profitability 14
Crafting a Revenue-Maximizing Business Model 18
    Creating a Value Proposition that Sells 18
    Pricing Strategies for Profitability 22
    Diversifying Revenue Streams 26
Enhancing the Member Experience 31
    Creating a Welcoming Environment 31
    Personalized Training and Support 35
    Leveraging Technology for Member Engagement 38
Building a Loyal Member Community 43
    The Power of Community in Fitness 43
    Hosting Events and Challenges 46
    Creating a Referral Program 50
Marketing Strategies for Growth and Retention 54
    Crafting a Compelling Brand Story 54
    Digital Marketing Tactics 58
    Measuring and Analyzing Marketing Success 63
Operational Excellence and Efficiency 69
    Streamlining Gym Operations 69

- Staff Training and Development 75
- Utilizing Data for Continuous Improvement 79
- Financial Management for Sustainable Growth 84
  - Budgeting and Financial Planning 84
  - Managing Cash Flow 88
  - Investment and Expansion Strategies 93
- Conclusion 99

Introduction

What if I told you that the secret to turning your gym into a thriving, profitable business lies not in acquiring more members, but in keeping the ones you already have? In an industry where new gyms seem to open on every corner, staying competitive isn't just about flashy marketing or the latest equipment. It's about understanding the true value of member retention and how maximizing the lifetime value of each customer can dramatically impact your bottom line. Imagine your gym not only packed with motivated members but also consistently growing, without the constant pressure of seeking new clients. That's the success formula we're going to explore.

This book is your guide to transforming your gym into a financial powerhouse by focusing on two critical pillars: boosting revenue and ensuring your members stick around for the long haul. Whether you're just starting out in the fitness business or you've been running your gym for years, the strategies in this book will help you unlock the full potential of your business.

At its core, this book serves one purpose: to equip you with actionable insights and proven strategies that will not only increase your gym's revenue but will also help you build a loyal, long-term member base. You'll learn how to create value that keeps people coming back, how to diversify your income streams, and how to optimize your operations to ensure sustained success. But this is more than just a guide for gym owners looking to make a quick buck—it's a blueprint for creating a gym that's built to last.

Why is this topic so important right now? Because the fitness industry is changing at a rapid pace. With the rise of boutique fitness centers, digital workout platforms, and an ever-growing number of competitors, gym owners are facing more pressure than ever to stand out. Meanwhile, consumer expectations are shifting. Today's members want more than just access to equipment—they want community, personalized experiences, and value that goes beyond their monthly fee. In this evolving landscape, the gyms that focus on delivering exceptional experiences and cultivating loyalty will be the ones that thrive.

My journey into the gym business began over a decade ago, and like many of you, I faced the uphill battle of trying to balance customer acquisition with retention, all while struggling to increase profitability. Through years of trial and error, I discovered that the real key to success wasn't found in continually chasing new members, but in fostering deeper relationships with those who had already chosen my gym. By focusing on retention, refining operational efficiency, and diversifying revenue streams, I turned a struggling facility into a thriving business. Now, I want to share that success formula with you.

The tone of this book is straightforward and practical, but also motivational. I want you to not only understand the strategies but feel empowered to put them into action. Running a successful gym is challenging, but with the right formula, it's absolutely achievable. You'll find real-world examples, tips from industry leaders, and actionable advice in each chapter, all designed to help you create a gym that's not just profitable but built to endure.

By the time you reach the final chapter, you'll have a clear roadmap for maximizing your revenue, keeping your members loyal, and ensuring your gym thrives for years to come. So, let's get started—your journey to gym business success begins here.

Chapter 1

Understanding the Gym Business Landscape

The Evolution of the Fitness Industry

The fitness industry has undergone an extraordinary transformation over the past few decades. What began as a niche activity for bodybuilders and athletes has grown into a global movement, catering to people from all walks of life. Today, fitness is as much about health, community, and well-being as it is about physical strength or appearance. Understanding how the industry has evolved can give you insight into where it's headed—and how your gym can position itself for success in this ever-changing landscape.

In the early days, the fitness industry was primarily dominated by hardcore gyms. Think back to the 1970s, when bodybuilding pioneers like Arnold Schwarzenegger made headlines and gold's gym became a cultural icon. These gyms catered to those who were serious about building muscle and physical prowess. Back then, fitness was about pushing limits and achieving peak physical form, mostly among a small group of dedicated individuals.

Fast forward to the 1980s, and the concept of fitness began to shift. With the rise of aerobic exercises and home workout videos—hello, Jane Fonda—fitness started becoming more accessible to the average person. The gym was no longer a place reserved for bodybuilders; it was now a welcoming environment for those simply looking to get in shape, lose weight, and improve their overall health. This era brought with it the first major wave of gym memberships, driven by a growing interest in personal wellness and the social aspect of group fitness classes.

As the 1990s rolled in, gyms evolved into more comprehensive fitness centers. These facilities offered a wider range of services, from group fitness classes to personal training and even nutrition counseling. This shift reflected the growing understanding that fitness was about more than just exercise—it was about an entire lifestyle. People started to view gyms as one-stop shops for their health and fitness needs. The big-box gyms, such as 24 Hour Fitness and LA Fitness, capitalized on this trend by offering a variety of equipment, services, and flexible membership plans that appealed to a broad audience.

The 2000s introduced a new wave of specialization within the fitness industry. Boutique fitness studios began popping up, offering focused experiences such as yoga, pilates, spinning, and functional training. These studios tapped into a desire for more personalized, community-driven fitness experiences, allowing members to feel part of a smaller, more intimate group rather than just a number in a large gym. The rise of CrossFit during this period is a prime example—what began as a grassroots movement quickly grew into a global phenomenon, demonstrating the power of niche fitness communities.

In the last decade, technology has become a major player in the fitness world. With the explosion of smartphones and wearables, fitness has gone digital. Apps, fitness trackers, and online platforms like Peloton and Apple Fitness+ now allow people to work out from the comfort of their own homes while staying connected to a larger community. The COVID-19 pandemic further accelerated this trend, forcing gyms and fitness businesses to adapt by offering online classes and hybrid memberships that combine in-person and virtual training. Today, consumers expect more flexibility in how and when they access fitness, whether that's through traditional gym memberships, online platforms, or a combination of both.

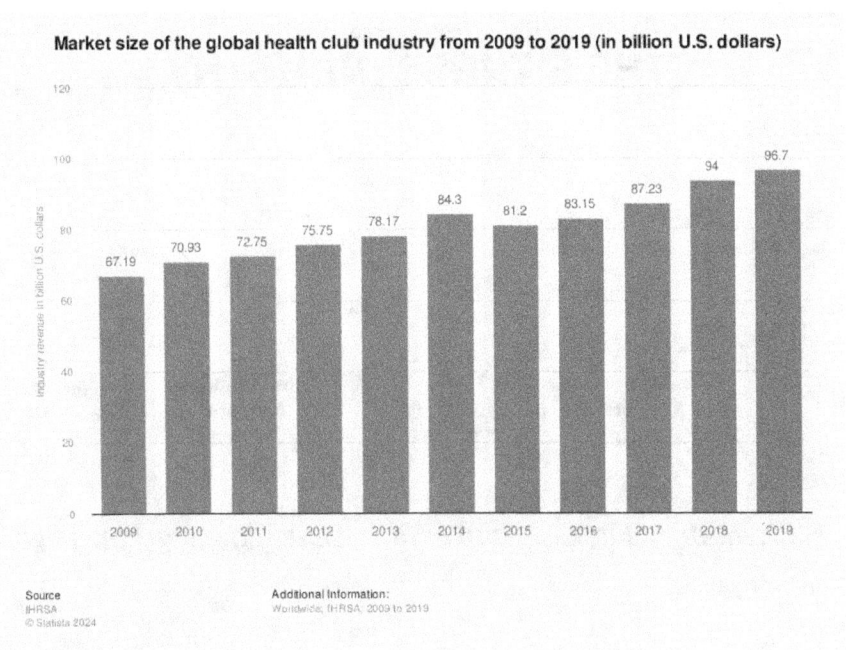

Growth of the Global Health Club Industry. Source: statista.com

The fitness industry's evolution is a story of continuous adaptation. What was once a niche market for bodybuilders has become a billion-dollar global industry that touches people's lives in deeply personal ways. As we move forward, the ability to adapt to trends like digital fitness, community-building, and personalized experiences will be crucial for any gym looking to succeed in this competitive space. Whether you run a large fitness center or a boutique studio, understanding this evolution gives you the context to innovate and meet your members' changing expectations.

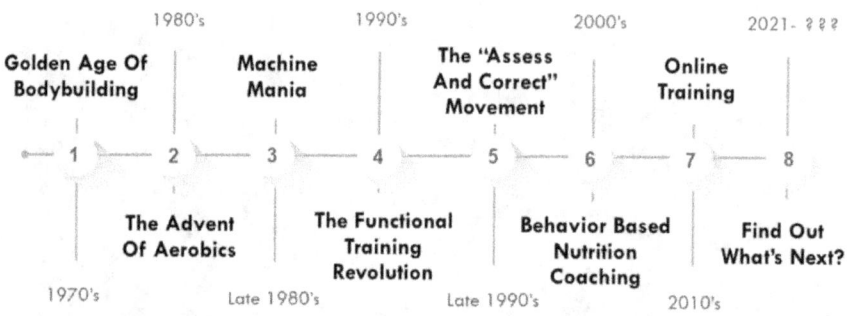

Evolution of Fitness. Source: fitnessmarketingmachine.net

Identifying Key Revenue Streams

In the gym business, it's crucial to understand where your income comes from. While the core of your revenue likely comes from memberships, there are many other potential sources that can significantly boost your profitability. By diversifying your revenue streams, you not only make your business more resilient but also open up new opportunities for growth.

Membership Fees: The Foundation

Membership fees are the backbone of any gym's revenue. Whether your model is a monthly subscription, annual membership, or pay-as-you-go option, these fees provide a consistent and reliable income. The key to maximizing this stream is offering different membership levels that cater to various customer needs. Some members might only want access to equipment, while others are looking for classes, personal training, or premium services like spa facilities or nutrition counseling. Offering tiered memberships not only provides flexibility but encourages people to upgrade to higher tiers as they see value in your offerings.

Personal Training: High-Value Upsell

Personal training is one of the most lucrative services a gym can offer. While many members are comfortable working out on their own, a significant number appreciate the guidance and motivation a personal trainer provides. Trainers can help with specific goals, whether it's weight loss, strength training, or recovering from an injury. Offering personal training as an upsell is an effective way to generate additional revenue. You can even provide specialized packages for different training types, such as group sessions or virtual coaching for those who can't make it to the gym.

A successful personal training program not only adds revenue but also increases member satisfaction and retention. People are more likely to stick with their fitness routines when they have personalized guidance and accountability, leading to longer-term memberships.

Group Classes: Building Community and Value

Group fitness classes are another excellent way to enhance your revenue. From yoga and Pilates to spin and HIIT (high-intensity interval training), group classes create a sense of community and make the gym experience more enjoyable for many members. This social aspect often keeps members coming back, which in turn improves retention rates. Additionally, offering a variety of classes at different times ensures that you're catering to all types of schedules and fitness preferences.

You can charge extra for certain specialized classes or include them as part of a premium membership package. Popular classes led by well-known instructors can even draw new members to your gym, particularly if they're marketed well.

Retail: Selling What Your Members Need

Many gyms overlook the potential of retail sales, but offering products that support fitness goals can be a profitable revenue stream. Think about what your members need during and after their workouts. Branded gym apparel, water bottles, yoga mats, and supplements like protein powders or energy bars are all items that members may find useful. By stocking a small retail area in your gym, you can increase convenience for members and add to your bottom line.

Keep in mind that the key to successful retail is offering products that align with your brand and resonate with your members. People are more likely to buy from you if they see a clear connection between the products and their fitness journey.

Additional Services: Expanding Your Offerings

There's also great potential in offering additional services that complement the gym experience. These can include massage therapy, nutrition consultations, or even recovery rooms with specialized equipment like compression boots or cryotherapy. Each of these services provides another way for you to engage your members and add to their overall experience, while simultaneously increasing revenue.

Expanding into these areas requires thoughtful planning and investment, but when done right, they can set your gym apart from the competition and create a more holistic wellness environment.

Events and Workshops: Engaging Your Members

Hosting events, workshops, and fitness challenges is a dynamic way to create engagement and generate extra income. You could organize boot camps, transformation challenges, or specialized workshops like self-defense or mindfulness seminars. These events not only provide an additional revenue stream but also deepen member loyalty by offering a sense of involvement and community.

Additionally, these types of events can be excellent marketing tools. Members are likely to bring friends or family along, which creates opportunities for guest passes, new memberships, and an overall boost in visibility for your gym.

Corporate Wellness Programs: A Steady Stream of Clients

One of the most overlooked revenue streams is partnering with local businesses to offer corporate wellness programs. Many companies are now recognizing the benefits of encouraging their employees to stay healthy, and gyms can capitalize on this by offering tailored wellness packages. These packages can include discounted memberships, group fitness sessions, or wellness seminars aimed at improving employee health.

By establishing relationships with businesses in your area, you can tap into a steady flow of new members and create a mutually beneficial arrangement that boosts your membership base while helping businesses support their employees' well-being.

By identifying and expanding key revenue streams, you create a more financially stable and profitable gym. Diversifying beyond traditional memberships—through services like personal training, group classes, retail sales, and corporate partnerships—not only increases revenue but also enhances member satisfaction and retention. A well-rounded business model ensures that your gym can thrive in an increasingly competitive industry.

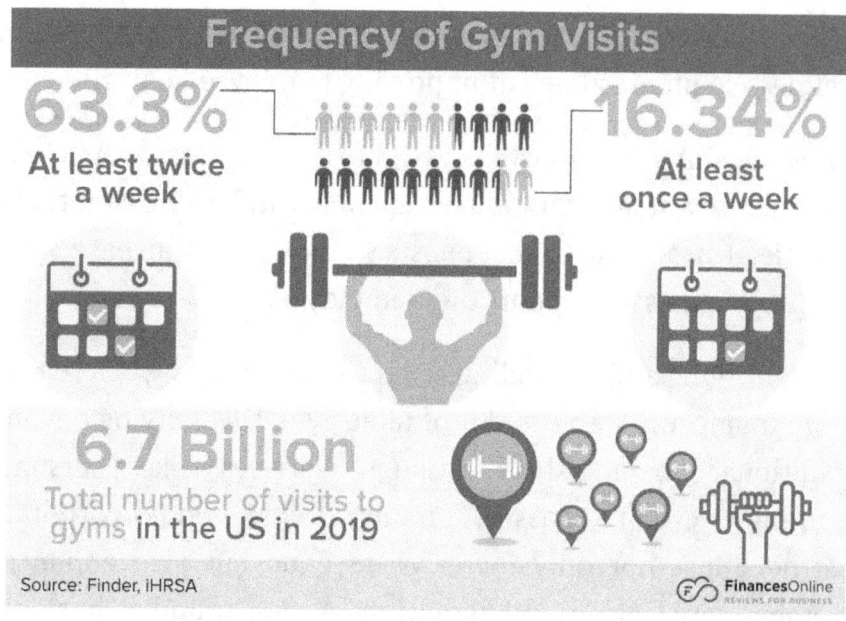

Frequency of Gym Visits in the U.S. Source: financesonline.com

The Role of Member Retention in Profitability

Member retention is the lifeblood of any gym's long-term success. While it's tempting to focus solely on bringing in new members, the real key to profitability lies in keeping the members you already have. Retaining members isn't just about maintaining a full gym floor—it's about creating a stable, reliable revenue stream that allows your business to thrive without the constant pressure of chasing new sign-ups.

The cost of acquiring new members is typically much higher than the cost of retaining existing ones. Think about the money spent on marketing campaigns, social media ads, and promotions designed to attract new faces. Each time a member leaves, you're essentially losing not just their membership fee but also the investment you made to bring them in. On the other hand, when a member stays with your gym for the long term, they provide ongoing revenue without the added costs of acquisition. This makes them far more valuable over time.

Beyond the financial advantages, retaining members also helps build a strong sense of community within your gym. Loyal members become advocates for your business. They're the ones who bring their friends to class, rave about your trainers, and leave glowing reviews online. Word-of-mouth marketing like this is incredibly powerful, and it's something that can't be bought. Happy, long-term members are more likely to participate in additional services your gym offers, whether it's personal training, group classes, or even merchandise. This not only boosts your revenue but also deepens their connection to your gym.

Member retention also provides stability, something every gym owner needs. When you can rely on a core group of loyal members, you don't have to scramble to replace the ones who leave. This stability allows you to plan more effectively for the future. You can invest in better equipment, offer more classes, and create a better overall experience because you know you have a solid foundation of members who aren't going anywhere.

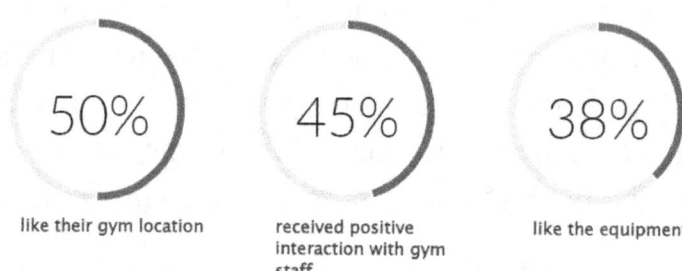

Top Motivators for Membership Retention. Source: financesonline.com

The key to great retention is understanding your members' needs and consistently delivering value. People stick around when they feel like they're getting more than just access to workout equipment—they want a sense of belonging, personalized attention, and a gym experience that fits seamlessly into their lives. When your gym becomes more than just a place to exercise, but a community that supports their goals, members are far less likely to leave.

Ultimately, retaining members isn't just good for business—it's the difference between a gym that struggles to survive and one that thrives. Every member you keep increases the lifetime value of your customer base, stabilizes your revenue, and sets your gym up for long-term success.

Chapter 2

Crafting a Revenue-Maximizing Business Model

Creating a Value Proposition that Sells

Your value proposition is the foundation of your gym's success. It's the promise you make to your members—the unique set of benefits they'll receive when they choose your gym over the competition. A compelling value proposition isn't just about listing what your gym offers; it's about highlighting why your gym is the best choice for your target audience.

At its core, your value proposition should clearly answer two important questions: **Why should someone join your gym?** and **What makes your gym different from the others?**

Know Your Audience

The first step in creating a value proposition that sells is understanding your audience. Are your potential members young professionals looking for convenience? Or are they older individuals seeking a low-impact workout environment? Different people look for different things in a gym, and a one-size-fits-all message won't work.

To create a value proposition that resonates, you need to put yourself in the shoes of your target market. Think about their needs, motivations, and fitness goals. For example, a gym that targets busy professionals might emphasize time efficiency—quick, effective workouts that fit into a hectic schedule. On the other hand, a gym focused on families might highlight a welcoming atmosphere with childcare options and family-friendly programming.

Highlight What Makes You Unique

Once you know who you're speaking to, the next step is identifying what makes your gym stand out. This is where you set yourself apart from the competition. What unique features or services does your gym offer that others don't? Maybe you have state-of-the-art equipment, highly certified trainers, or specialized classes like boxing or hot yoga.

It could even be something less tangible, like the atmosphere of your gym. Perhaps your members feel like part of a community, or maybe your gym is known for its friendly, approachable staff. These are the kinds of factors that can make a difference to someone choosing between your gym and the one down the street.

Focus on the specific benefits your members get, rather than just listing features. For instance, instead of saying, "We offer personal training," frame it in terms of the benefit: "Achieve your fitness goals faster with personalized, one-on-one coaching." The more clearly you can connect what you offer with what your members truly care about, the stronger your value proposition will be.

Keep It Simple and Clear

A value proposition should be simple, direct, and easy to understand. Avoid jargon or complicated language. You want prospective members to immediately grasp what your gym offers and why it matters. Keep your value proposition short and to the point—ideally, it should be one or two sentences that capture the essence of your gym.

For example: "At FitPro Gym, we offer tailored fitness programs and personalized coaching in a supportive, results-driven environment. Whether you're a beginner or a seasoned athlete, we help you meet your goals, your way."

A clear, concise message like this communicates exactly what potential members can expect without overwhelming them with too much information.

Back It Up with Proof

Once you've nailed down your value proposition, it's essential to make sure it's backed by action. Your value proposition is a promise, and delivering on that promise is what builds trust and keeps members coming back. If you claim to have the best trainers in town, ensure that your trainers are not only certified but continuously improving and engaging with members. If your gym is all about community, create opportunities for members to connect through events, challenges, or social gatherings.

A strong value proposition is much more powerful when members see the proof in their daily experience. Happy, satisfied members become your best advocates, spreading the word about your gym and reinforcing the promises you make.

Evolving Your Value Proposition

Finally, remember that your value proposition isn't set in stone. As the fitness industry changes and your gym grows, you may need to refine your message to keep it relevant. Regularly assess what's working and what's not—both in terms of your services and how you communicate your value to potential members. Your ability to adapt and evolve will ensure that your gym remains competitive and continues to attract new members.

Creating a value proposition that sells is about more than just clever marketing. It's about clearly defining the benefits your gym offers, making them irresistible to your target audience, and delivering on the promises you make every single day.

Pricing Strategies for Profitability

Setting the right pricing strategy is one of the most important decisions you'll make as a gym owner. Your prices not only need to cover costs and generate profit but also reflect the value of the experience you're offering to members. The challenge is striking the right balance between being competitive in the market and ensuring your gym remains financially healthy.

The first step in building a profitable pricing strategy is understanding your costs. This includes everything from rent, equipment, and utilities to payroll, marketing, and maintenance. Knowing your overhead is essential because your pricing needs to cover these expenses while still leaving room for profit. However, pricing isn't just about covering costs—it's also about positioning your gym in a way that aligns with your target market. A boutique gym offering specialized classes and personal training should price differently than a large commercial gym with basic equipment and minimal frills.

One common mistake many gym owners make is underpricing in an effort to attract more members. While offering lower prices might get people through the door, it can lead to long-term challenges. Low prices can devalue your services and make it difficult to raise rates in the future. Instead, consider positioning your gym as a premium experience where members are willing to pay more for the added value you provide—whether it's personalized attention, cutting-edge equipment, or a sense of community.

Offering tiered pricing is an effective way to appeal to different segments of your market while maintaining profitability. For example, you might offer a basic membership that includes access to gym equipment and facilities, a mid-tier membership that includes group fitness classes, and a premium membership that offers additional perks such as personal training or access to exclusive events. This approach allows you to cater to budget-conscious members while maximizing revenue from those willing to pay for more personalized or comprehensive services.

Another strategy is to create membership packages that reward long-term commitment. Offering discounts for members who sign up for longer periods, such as six months or a year, can help ensure a steady cash flow and reduce the risk of member churn.

These packages can provide stability for your business and incentivize members to stay longer, reducing the need for constant re-marketing.

In addition to monthly or annual memberships, consider offering flexible pricing options like drop-in rates, class passes, or punch cards. These options can attract people who may not be ready to commit to a full membership but are interested in trying out your gym. While these short-term options don't generate the same consistent income as memberships, they provide an opportunity to convert occasional visitors into long-term members over time.

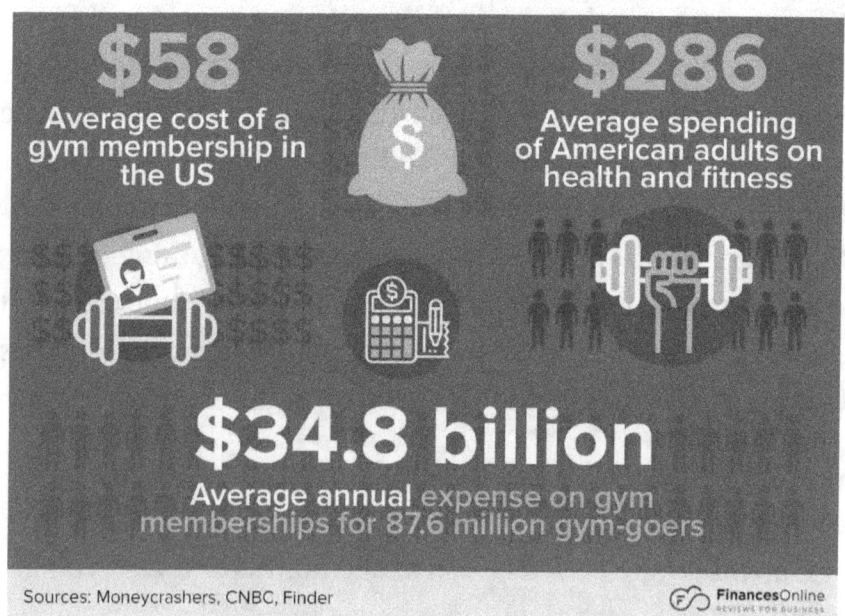

Breakdown of Fitness Costs in the U.S. Source: financesonline.com

Ultimately, the key to a successful pricing strategy is ensuring that your members feel they're getting value for what they're paying. If your prices reflect the quality of service, the community, and the overall experience your gym offers, members will be more likely to see your gym as an investment in their health rather than just another expense. With the right pricing approach, you can ensure profitability while still delivering a great experience that keeps members coming back.

Diversifying Revenue Streams

Running a gym isn't just about selling memberships anymore. While membership fees are a crucial part of your income, relying solely on them can limit your potential. To make your business more profitable and sustainable, it's important to explore multiple revenue streams. This not only boosts your income but also protects your business from the ups and downs of membership fluctuations. The more diverse your revenue, the stronger your financial foundation becomes.

Personal Training and Coaching

Personal training is one of the easiest ways to increase revenue without needing a lot of extra space or equipment. Many members are willing to pay extra for the one-on-one attention that a personal trainer provides. Whether they want help with their form, personalized workout plans, or motivation to reach their goals, personal training adds significant value. Offering various packages—such as one-on-one sessions, small group training, or even virtual coaching—gives you flexibility in pricing and appeal to different types of members.

A successful personal training program can also lead to better member retention. When members feel supported and see real progress, they're more likely to stick around.

Specialized Classes and Programs

Group fitness classes are another great way to diversify your revenue. Classes like yoga, Pilates, spinning, or high-intensity interval training (HIIT) often attract people who enjoy working out in a social setting. These classes can be included as part of a premium membership or offered as an additional paid service. The key is offering a variety of classes that appeal to different fitness levels and interests.

Additionally, offering specialized programs like boot camps, weight loss challenges, or sports-specific training can draw in new clients who might not be interested in a standard membership but are excited about a particular program.

Retail and Merchandise

Selling merchandise is another often underutilized way to generate revenue. Your members need workout gear, supplements, and other fitness-related products, and they're often willing to purchase them from a place they trust—your gym. Stocking items like branded clothing, protein shakes, water bottles, and yoga mats can not only generate extra income but also build a stronger connection between your brand and your members. When someone wears your gym's logo, it's free advertising that can also attract new members.

To make retail successful, focus on offering products that align with your members' needs and preferences. It's not about having a wide selection, but rather providing high-quality, useful items that your members are excited to buy.

Online Training and Virtual Services

The shift to online fitness during recent years has opened up a whole new revenue stream. Offering virtual training programs, on-demand workout videos, or live-streamed classes can extend your gym's reach beyond its physical location. This can appeal to members who prefer to work out from home, travel frequently, or want flexibility in their schedule.

Online services are also scalable—you can create a library of workout content that members can access for a monthly subscription or as part of a premium membership. Virtual personal training is another growing trend, allowing trainers to work with clients one-on-one through video sessions, opening up new possibilities without needing extra physical space.

Partnerships and Corporate Wellness Programs

Forming partnerships with local businesses is another way to increase your revenue. Many companies are now investing in employee wellness programs, and gyms can play a key role in this effort. You can create customized wellness packages for businesses, offering group memberships, fitness classes, or even wellness workshops. This provides a steady flow of clients while also improving your community presence.

Additionally, partnering with local health-related businesses like chiropractors, nutritionists, or massage therapists can help you offer more comprehensive services. These partnerships can result in mutual referrals, adding value for your members while generating new business.

Additional Wellness Services

Expanding into wellness services like massage therapy, nutrition counseling, or physical therapy adds another dimension to your gym's offerings. These services appeal to members who are looking to improve their overall health, not just their fitness. You could offer these services as part of a membership package or as an add-on, creating more opportunities for revenue.

The key to successfully diversifying your revenue streams is to understand your members' needs and offer services that complement their fitness journey. When done thoughtfully, each additional stream not only boosts income but also enhances the value your gym provides, making it a place where members get everything they need to succeed.

Chapter 3

Enhancing the Member Experience

Creating a Welcoming Environment

When someone walks into your gym for the first time, their initial impression shapes how they feel about the space and whether they want to become a member. Creating a welcoming environment isn't just about having clean floors or modern equipment; it's about making people feel comfortable, supported, and valued from the moment they step through the door.

A welcoming environment starts with the physical space. Lighting, layout, and cleanliness all play a big role in setting the tone for your gym. Bright, well-lit spaces feel open and inviting, while poorly lit areas can feel cramped or unwelcoming. How your gym is organized also matters. Clear signage, intuitive flow between workout zones, and ample space for movement can make a big difference in how your gym feels to both new visitors and long-time members.

Modern Gym Entrance. Source: landmarksarchitects.com

But beyond the aesthetics, the atmosphere of your gym is largely shaped by the people within it—your staff and your members. When your staff is friendly, approachable, and genuinely interested in helping members achieve their goals, it creates a positive, supportive culture that encourages people to stick around. A simple "hello" at the front desk or a personal check-in from a trainer can go a long way in making someone feel welcome. Building these personal connections is key to making your gym more than just a place to work out. It becomes a place where people feel they belong.

The vibe your gym creates also plays a big role in its overall feel. Music, for example, can set the mood for your space. Upbeat tunes can energize members, while more relaxing playlists might work better in a yoga studio or quiet corner for stretching. Paying attention to these little details shows that you care about the overall experience, not just the workout itself.

Modern Gym Interior. Source: gymflow.io

Inclusivity is another crucial element of creating a welcoming environment. Everyone, regardless of their fitness level, background, or body type, should feel comfortable in your gym.

This means fostering an atmosphere where members feel free to be themselves without fear of judgment. You can achieve this by offering a wide range of classes or equipment for all skill levels, as well as promoting diversity within your staff. Having trainers and instructors from different backgrounds creates a sense of representation that resonates with your members.

It's also important to remember that for many people, walking into a gym can be an intimidating experience, especially if they're new to fitness. You can help ease these nerves by making your gym's culture approachable. For instance, offer beginner-friendly classes, host new member orientations, or provide resources that help people get started without feeling overwhelmed. When people feel supported, they're more likely to stick with their fitness journey—and your gym.

Ultimately, a welcoming environment is one where members feel like they're part of a community. When people feel valued, supported, and at ease in your gym, they're not only more likely to come back—they're also more likely to tell their friends about the great experience they've had. By focusing on creating this kind of positive atmosphere, you're setting your gym up for long-term success.

Personalized Training and Support

One of the most effective ways to keep your gym members engaged and motivated is by offering personalized training and support. People are more likely to stay committed to their fitness goals when they feel like their unique needs and progress are being noticed. Personalized training adds real value to your members' experience by making them feel seen, supported, and encouraged on their journey.

Tailored Workout Plans

Not all gym members are the same. Some are just starting out and may feel overwhelmed, while others might be more advanced and looking for ways to push themselves harder. Personalized workout plans cater to these individual needs, giving each member a clear path to follow based on their fitness level, goals, and even their preferences.

When you take the time to create custom workout plans, you're showing members that you're invested in their success. For beginners, a plan that introduces them to basic exercises and helps them build confidence is crucial. For more experienced members, plans that include challenging routines, performance tracking, and even access to advanced classes can keep them engaged and striving for more.

Ongoing Progress Monitoring

Once you've designed a personalized plan, the next step is to track each member's progress. This is where ongoing support really comes into play. Regular check-ins, progress assessments, and adjustments to the workout routine based on results help members stay on track and feel motivated. It's important to celebrate their successes—whether that's a personal best in weightlifting or simply sticking with their routine for a month straight.

Having personal trainers or staff members regularly monitor and engage with members about their progress adds a sense of accountability, which can significantly improve retention. When members feel like someone cares about their progress, they're more likely to stick around and keep working toward their goals.

Adapting to Individual Preferences

Personalized training isn't just about fitness levels—it's also about preferences. Some people enjoy intense workouts, while others prefer a more relaxed, low-impact approach. Catering to these preferences ensures that your members stay engaged and don't lose interest.

For example, offering different workout styles—like high-intensity interval training for those who love to push hard, or yoga and Pilates for members who prioritize flexibility and balance—can make your gym a place where everyone feels comfortable. This level of personalization helps members feel like the gym is genuinely aligned with their needs and interests.

Building Stronger Relationships

Personalized training goes beyond just workouts; it's about building relationships with your members. When a trainer or staff member takes the time to get to know someone, understand their goals, and guide them through their fitness journey, it creates a sense of trust and loyalty.

Members who feel connected to their trainers or gym staff are much more likely to stay long-term. They're not just coming in for a workout—they're coming in because they feel like they belong. This sense of belonging is key to member retention, as it transforms your gym into a supportive community rather than just a place to exercise.

Offering personalized training and support is about creating a relationship with each member and helping them feel like they're on a path that's made specifically for them. It's a powerful way to enhance the gym experience and keep people coming back, eager to continue their fitness journey with your guidance.

Leveraging Technology for Member Engagement

Technology has transformed how people approach fitness, and gyms that effectively integrate it into their operations can significantly enhance member engagement. Whether it's through apps, wearables, or social media, technology can provide your members with tools that motivate them, track their progress, and keep them connected to your gym, even when they're not physically there.

Fitness Apps and Tracking

One of the most impactful ways to engage your members is through fitness apps that allow them to track their workouts, set goals, and monitor progress. Many gyms now offer branded apps that sync with their equipment or provide members with a way to log their exercises, whether they're at the gym or at home. These apps often include features like workout plans, class schedules, and progress charts, giving members the ability to manage their fitness journey all in one place.

By providing an app with these capabilities, you're offering more than just a gym membership—you're giving members a personalized fitness tool that they can use every day. This adds value to their membership and helps keep them motivated. When members can see their progress and easily access workout information, they're more likely to stay engaged and consistent with their routine.

Wearables and Data Integration

Wearable fitness devices, such as smartwatches and fitness trackers, are another key piece of technology that can help drive member engagement. Many people already use these devices to monitor their activity, and gyms that incorporate wearables into their programming can create an even more immersive experience.

For example, wearables can track heart rate, steps, calories burned, and more. When you integrate this data into your gym's ecosystem, it allows members to see how their in-gym workouts contribute to their overall fitness. Some gyms offer challenges or competitions based on wearable data, encouraging members to hit certain fitness milestones or compete with friends for fun rewards.

Wearables also offer trainers a window into their clients' performance and recovery. By reviewing the data, trainers can make informed adjustments to workout plans, ensuring that members are making progress and staying safe. This level of personalization, powered by data, helps members feel supported and connected.

Virtual Classes and On-Demand Workouts

The rise of virtual classes and on-demand workouts has opened up a new avenue for keeping members engaged, even when they can't make it to the gym. Offering a variety of virtual classes, such as yoga, strength training, or cardio, allows members to maintain their fitness routines from home or while traveling. On-demand options give members the flexibility to work out on their schedule, rather than having to attend a class at a specific time.

This convenience is highly valued, especially by members with busy lives. Virtual options not only keep members active but also reinforce their connection to your gym, as they continue to engage with your brand even when they aren't physically present. Regularly updating the class offerings keeps the content fresh and exciting, ensuring that members always have something new to try.

Most Popular Virtual Fitness Classes. Source: financesonline.com

Social Media Engagement

Social media is another powerful tool for fostering member engagement. Platforms like Instagram, Facebook, and TikTok can be used to build a sense of community around your gym. Sharing member success stories, workout tips, and motivational content helps keep your gym top of mind and creates a deeper connection with your members.

Encouraging members to share their own workout journeys or tag your gym in their posts can further strengthen this sense of community. Offering challenges or contests on social media, where members can win prizes for participation, adds a fun, interactive element to their fitness experience. The more engaged your members feel with your gym's online presence, the more likely they are to stay loyal and involved.

Leveraging technology effectively allows your gym to stay connected with members in more meaningful ways, both inside and outside of the physical space. This constant engagement helps build stronger relationships and keeps members motivated, ensuring they see your gym as an essential part of their fitness journey.

Chapter 4

Building a Loyal Member Community

The Power of Community in Fitness

A sense of community can be one of the most powerful drivers behind the success of a gym. People often come for the workouts, but they stay for the relationships and the feeling of belonging. When members feel like they're part of something bigger than just their fitness routine, they become more engaged and motivated. Building a strong community within your gym can not only enhance the member experience but also significantly improve retention.

Creating a Supportive Environment

One of the reasons community is so important in fitness is that it provides a built-in support system. Many people struggle to stay consistent with their fitness goals, especially when life gets busy or progress seems slow. However, being part of a community where everyone is working toward similar goals can provide the encouragement and motivation that keeps members on track.

In a gym setting, this might look like members cheering each other on during a workout, trainers offering encouragement, or people sharing their progress and challenges. The more supportive the environment, the more likely it is that members will feel a personal connection to the gym and their fitness journey.

Fostering Relationships Between Members

Gyms that foster relationships between members create a social bond that goes beyond exercise. When people feel like they know each other, they're more likely to keep coming back—not just for the workout, but for the sense of camaraderie. Group fitness classes are a natural way to build these connections, as they bring people together in a shared experience.

Outside of classes, organizing social events like fitness challenges, charity runs, or member appreciation nights can deepen these relationships. These events allow members to get to know each other in a relaxed setting, which strengthens the sense of community. As these connections grow, members will start to see the gym as more than just a place to work out. It becomes a place where they feel a sense of belonging.

Motivation Through Accountability

A strong gym community also provides a sense of accountability. When members build friendships with others in the gym, they often feel a greater responsibility to show up, not just for themselves but for the people they've connected with. This accountability helps create a routine, making it easier for members to stay consistent with their fitness goals.

Knowing that their workout partners or classmates will notice if they skip a session can be a powerful motivator. It turns the gym into a place where people look forward to being, not just because of the workout but because they know they'll be missed if they don't show up.

Shared Goals and Collective Energy

When people work out in a group or as part of a community, the collective energy can be contagious. Seeing others push through challenges can inspire members to do the same. It creates a positive cycle of motivation, where each person's effort fuels the group.

Gyms that tap into this shared energy often find that their members are more motivated, committed, and excited about their fitness goals. Whether it's through friendly competition or shared milestones, being part of a fitness community helps members feel like they're on a journey with others, making the process more enjoyable and fulfilling.

The power of community in fitness goes beyond just creating a friendly atmosphere—it transforms the gym experience. When members feel connected, supported, and encouraged by those around them, they're more likely to stay dedicated to their fitness goals and, in turn, remain loyal to your gym.

Hosting Events and Challenges

Hosting events and fitness challenges is one of the most effective ways to energize your gym community and keep members engaged. These activities not only add excitement to the gym routine but also foster a sense of connection among members. When done right, events and challenges can boost member retention, attract new clients, and create a fun, motivating environment that keeps people coming back.

Creating a Sense of Community

Events and challenges give members an opportunity to connect with each other in ways they might not during a regular workout. Whether it's a friendly competition or a collaborative event, these gatherings create a sense of belonging that is often missing in solo workouts. When members feel like they're part of a supportive community, they're more likely to stick with their fitness routines and remain loyal to your gym.

Hosting events such as open house days, fitness expos, or wellness workshops can also draw in potential new members. These are great opportunities to showcase your gym's unique culture and offerings, allowing people to experience what sets you apart.

For existing members, events like these break up the routine and offer a chance to engage in different aspects of health and fitness that they might not have considered before. It can be something as simple as a nutrition seminar or as engaging as a member appreciation day with guest instructors and fun activities.

Fitness Challenges for Motivation

Challenges are a powerful way to motivate your members and keep them committed to their fitness goals. A well-designed challenge taps into both individual drive and the energy of competition, which can help push people to go beyond their comfort zones.

Challenges can be structured around various themes, like weight loss, endurance, strength, or even consistency. For example, a 30-day challenge where participants aim to complete a certain number of workouts or meet specific fitness goals can create a buzz in the gym. To make these challenges more engaging, you can incorporate milestones or offer small rewards as members make progress, whether it's achieving a personal best in a class or logging the most hours in the gym.

These challenges can be as simple or as elaborate as you want. The key is to make them fun and accessible to everyone, regardless of their fitness level. When members see real results from their participation—whether that's improving their fitness or just feeling part of something bigger—it reinforces their commitment to the gym.

Leveraging Competitions and Social Events

Competitions can add a layer of excitement and friendly rivalry to the gym experience. Events like fitness competitions, obstacle courses, or even themed workout contests can bring out the competitive spirit in your members. These types of events are not only great for fostering community but can also be a lot of fun, keeping people interested and engaged in the long term.

You don't always need a serious competition to engage members. Social events, such as group hikes, team-building workouts, or fitness-themed parties, can build camaraderie among members in a more relaxed atmosphere. These kinds of events are a way to celebrate fitness while allowing people to connect outside of their usual workout routines. They make the gym experience more than just about exercise—it becomes a place where friendships and lasting bonds are formed.

Keeping Events Fresh and Inclusive

The success of hosting events and challenges lies in keeping things fresh and inclusive. Rotate the types of challenges and events you offer throughout the year so members are always looking forward to something new. A seasonal calendar filled with different events—like holiday-themed challenges, summer boot camps, or spring fitness festivals—keeps engagement levels high and prevents monotony.

Inclusivity is also key. When planning events and challenges, consider your entire member base. Make sure that the activities are suitable for various fitness levels and encourage participation from both newcomers and seasoned athletes. Offering different tiers or modifying challenges can ensure that everyone feels welcome to join in.

Hosting events and challenges transforms your gym from a place where people just work out into a lively, connected community. They provide members with new goals, new friendships, and a sense of accomplishment that extends beyond individual workouts.

Creating a Referral Program

A well-designed referral program can be one of the most effective ways to grow your gym membership. When current members are happy with their experience, they naturally want to share it with friends and family. By providing a simple, attractive referral program, you can encourage them to do just that. Not only does this help bring in new members, but it also strengthens your relationship with your existing ones by rewarding them for their loyalty.

Incentivizing Referrals

The key to any successful referral program is offering an incentive that appeals to your members. People are more likely to refer someone if they feel there's a meaningful reward involved. This could be a free month of membership, discounted personal training sessions, or even branded merchandise like gym apparel or equipment.

However, the reward doesn't always have to be large. Sometimes, even smaller gestures like a guest pass or a gift card can motivate members to refer others. The important thing is to make the incentive valuable enough that members feel appreciated for their effort. Think about what your particular membership base values most and tailor the rewards accordingly.

Making It Simple and Easy to Use

For a referral program to be effective, it must be easy to use. Members should be able to refer a friend without having to go through a complicated process. The more barriers you remove, the more likely people are to participate.

One approach is to create a simple referral link that members can share through email, text, or social media. Alternatively, you could provide referral cards that members can hand out. Whatever method you choose, make sure it's straightforward and accessible.

It's also important to clearly communicate how the program works. Let members know exactly what they need to do and what they'll receive in return. When the process is simple and well-explained, participation will naturally increase.

Recognizing Referrals Publicly

Another powerful aspect of a referral program is public recognition. People like to be acknowledged, especially in front of their peers. Recognizing members who bring in new referrals can boost participation and foster a sense of community. You could display a referral leaderboard in your gym, mention top referrers in a newsletter, or give a shout-out on social media.

This public recognition not only rewards members but also encourages others to get involved. It adds a level of friendly competition that can drive even more referrals. Plus, it reinforces the idea that your gym values its members and their contributions.

Offering a Benefit to New Members

A referral program works best when it benefits both the referring member and the new member they bring in. Offering a special deal to the person being referred, like a discounted membership or a free introductory class, makes it more enticing for new people to join. It also creates a win-win scenario where both parties feel like they're getting something valuable.

This benefit for new members can serve as a great icebreaker, making their decision to join easier and more appealing. Plus, when someone knows they're getting a good deal through a trusted friend's referral, they're more likely to feel confident in their choice to join your gym.

Tracking and Adjusting the Program

To ensure your referral program is successful, it's important to track its performance. Pay attention to how many new members are coming in through referrals and whether the program is meeting your expectations. Over time, you may need to make adjustments—whether that means changing the rewards, simplifying the process, or increasing awareness of the program.

The success of a referral program often depends on how well it fits your gym's community. Keep an open mind, listen to feedback from your members, and fine-tune the details to keep the program fresh and engaging. When done right, a referral program can be one of the most cost-effective ways to grow your membership while building a stronger, more connected community.

Chapter 5

Marketing Strategies for Growth and Retention

Crafting a Compelling Brand Story

Every gym needs more than just great equipment and classes to stand out—it needs a compelling brand story. Your brand story is what gives your gym personality, purpose, and a connection to your members. It's the narrative that explains why your gym exists, what it stands for, and how it makes a difference in people's lives. A well-crafted brand story goes beyond just marketing; it resonates with your audience on a personal level and helps build loyalty.

Start with Your "Why"

The foundation of any great brand story is the reason why your gym exists. What motivated you to open a gym in the first place? Was it a passion for fitness, a desire to help others live healthier lives, or maybe an inspiring personal journey? The "why" behind your gym gives it heart and makes it relatable to potential members. People are drawn to businesses with a clear purpose, especially when that purpose aligns with their own values or goals.

For example, if your gym was started because you wanted to create a space where people of all fitness levels feel welcome and supported, that becomes the heart of your brand story. It's not just about the equipment or the classes—it's about fostering an inclusive environment where everyone can achieve their goals.

Highlight the Journey

Once you've established why your gym exists, consider sharing the journey that brought it to life. People love stories of perseverance, growth, and overcoming challenges. Whether it's the struggle of opening your doors for the first time or the hurdles you've overcome to create a successful community, these moments make your brand more human and relatable.

Your journey doesn't need to be grand or dramatic—authenticity is what matters most. Sharing the ups and downs of building your gym shows potential members that you've worked hard to create something meaningful, and that effort speaks volumes about the quality of experience they can expect.

Connect with Your Audience's Aspirations

A compelling brand story isn't just about your gym—it's about how your gym connects to the lives of your members. Think about what your audience aspires to achieve. Are they looking to transform their health, boost their confidence, or find a community of like-minded individuals? Your story should reflect these desires and show how your gym can help make them a reality.

For instance, if many of your members are busy professionals struggling to balance fitness with their hectic lives, your brand story could focus on how your gym offers efficient, effective workouts that fit seamlessly into their schedule. Show them that you understand their challenges and have designed your gym to meet their specific needs.

Showcase Your Values

What does your gym stand for? Your core values are a key part of your brand story and help define the culture and experience you provide. Maybe your gym is all about inclusivity, innovation, or personal growth. Whatever your values are, they should be woven into the narrative you create around your brand.

For example, if inclusivity is a cornerstone of your gym, your brand story might focus on how you've built a welcoming space for people of all backgrounds and fitness levels. You could highlight how your gym goes the extra mile to make sure every member feels comfortable and supported, no matter where they are in their fitness journey.

By clearly articulating your values, you attract members who share those beliefs and are looking for a gym that aligns with what's important to them.

Be Authentic and Human

Above all, your brand story needs to be authentic. People can sense when a story is forced or disingenuous, so it's important to stay true to who you are and what your gym is really about. Share your story in a way that feels natural, not overly polished or scripted.

Don't be afraid to inject personality into your brand story. If your gym is known for its fun, energetic atmosphere, let that energy shine through in your narrative. If you take a more down-to-earth, supportive approach, make sure your story reflects that tone. The more human your brand feels, the easier it will be for people to connect with it.

A well-crafted brand story helps potential members understand what makes your gym special and why they should be a part of it. It's not just about what you offer; it's about the experience and community you've created. When your story resonates, it becomes more than just marketing—it becomes the reason people choose your gym over others and stay loyal for years to come.

Digital Marketing Tactics

Digital marketing is an essential tool for growing your gym's presence and attracting new members. With so many people turning to online platforms to research businesses, it's important to have a strong digital strategy that reaches your audience where they spend most of their time. By leveraging the right tactics, you can increase your gym's visibility, engage potential members, and keep current ones connected.

Social Media Engagement

Social media is one of the most powerful ways to connect with your audience. Platforms like Instagram, Facebook, and even TikTok offer gyms the chance to showcase their culture, promote their services, and interact directly with potential members. The key to social media marketing is consistency and authenticity. Posting regularly about what's happening at your gym—whether it's a new class, a member success story, or a behind-the-scenes look at your trainers—helps create a dynamic and engaging presence.

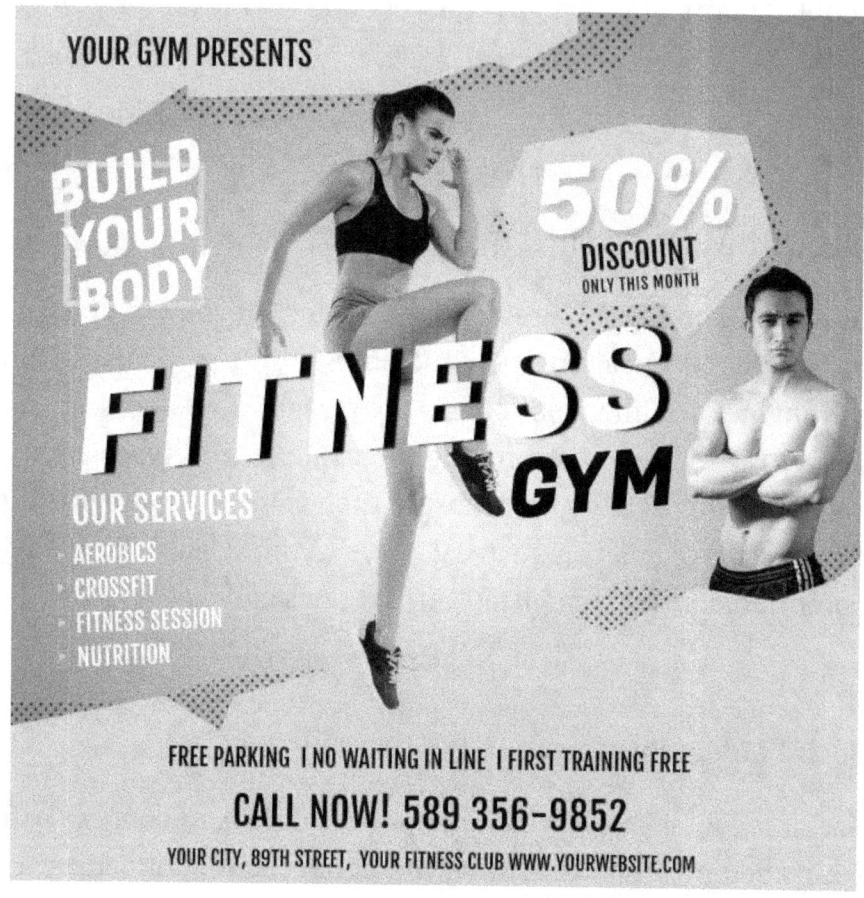

Social Media Post Example. Source: postermywall.com

It's important to not just post, but also engage with your audience. Reply to comments, answer questions, and show appreciation for members who tag your gym in their posts. This interaction builds a sense of community and keeps your gym top-of-mind. It also gives potential members a glimpse of what it feels like to be part of your gym, which can be a big motivator for them to join.

Email Campaigns

Email marketing is another highly effective digital tool that often gets overlooked. A well-crafted email campaign can keep current members informed and engaged while also nurturing leads who may be interested in joining. Emails can be used to send updates on new classes, promote special offers, or share helpful fitness tips. Personalized emails that address a member by name or provide content based on their preferences can make your outreach feel more meaningful and less like generic advertising.

It's also a good idea to create a regular newsletter that shares stories from your gym community, upcoming events, and fitness advice. This helps you stay connected with your members and keeps your gym at the forefront of their minds, even when they're not working out.

Search Engine Optimization (SEO)

Making sure your gym's website ranks well in search engines is crucial for attracting local members. People often search online when looking for a gym near them, and if your website isn't optimized, you could miss out on potential traffic. SEO involves optimizing your website's content to ensure it appears in search results when people look for gyms in your area.

You can start by including local keywords—like "gym in [your city]" or "personal training in [your area]"—throughout your site's pages, blog posts, and even in your page titles. Additionally, creating content that answers common questions or provides valuable information about fitness will help improve your site's search ranking. The more visible your gym is online, the more likely people are to discover it when they're ready to join.

Paid Advertising

While organic reach is important, investing in paid digital advertising can accelerate your gym's growth. Platforms like Facebook, Instagram, and Google Ads allow you to target specific audiences based on demographics, location, and even interests. For example, you can run ads that only show to people who live within a certain radius of your gym or those who are interested in fitness and wellness.

Well-designed ads with a strong call to action—like a limited-time offer for a free trial or a discounted membership—can be incredibly effective at bringing in new leads. The key is to create ads that are visually appealing and directly speak to the needs of your target audience. Regularly tracking and adjusting your ads based on performance will ensure that your investment is paying off.

Content Marketing

Content marketing is about providing valuable, informative content that showcases your expertise and helps potential members solve problems or achieve their goals. This could be through blog posts, videos, or even downloadable guides. For example, you might write blog articles about the benefits of strength training or post a video series that teaches proper workout techniques.

By sharing useful content, you position your gym as a trusted resource in the fitness community. This not only helps with SEO but also builds trust with your audience, making them more likely to choose your gym when they're ready to commit to a fitness routine.

Online Reviews and Testimonials

Positive reviews can have a big impact on your gym's reputation. Many potential members look at online reviews before deciding to join a gym, so encouraging your current members to leave positive feedback can go a long way. Highlighting testimonials on your website and social media also shows potential members that real people are finding success at your gym.

Responding to reviews—both positive and negative—demonstrates that you care about your members' experiences and are committed to providing excellent service. This interaction can also build credibility and trust, making it more likely that new people will choose your gym.

Measuring and Analyzing Marketing Success

When it comes to growing your gym business, marketing plays a crucial role. But simply running ads or posting on social media isn't enough. To truly understand whether your marketing efforts are working, you need to measure and analyze their success. This allows you to see what's driving results and where there's room for improvement, so you can adjust your strategy and maximize your return on investment (ROI).

Track Your Key Metrics

The first step in measuring marketing success is identifying the right metrics to track. These key performance indicators (KPIs) will give you a clear picture of how your efforts are performing. For most gyms, these might include:

- **New Member Sign-Ups**: How many new members have joined since you launched a campaign?

- **Lead Generation**: How many people are showing interest by signing up for free trials, joining mailing lists, or inquiring about membership?

- **Website Traffic**: Are more people visiting your website as a result of your marketing efforts?

- **Conversion Rate**: Out of the people who engage with your marketing (click an ad, visit the website, etc.), how many actually sign up for a membership?

By focusing on these metrics, you can get a clearer sense of whether your campaigns are bringing in new business.

Understand the Source of Your Traffic

Not all marketing channels will perform equally, so it's important to analyze where your traffic and new members are coming from. If you're running multiple campaigns across different platforms—social media, email marketing, Google ads, or community partnerships—you need to know which are driving the best results.

Tools like Google Analytics can help track the source of your website traffic, showing whether people are finding you through organic search, paid ads, social media, or other channels. If a particular platform is performing better than others, it makes sense to invest more resources there. On the other hand, if a certain channel isn't yielding results, you may want to rethink how you're using it or shift your focus elsewhere.

Calculate Your Customer Acquisition Cost

Another important metric is your **customer acquisition cost (CAC)**—the amount of money you're spending to bring in each new member. To calculate this, take the total amount you've spent on a marketing campaign and divide it by the number of new members it brought in.

For example, if you spent $1,000 on an ad campaign and gained 10 new members, your CAC would be $100 per member. Comparing your CAC across different campaigns can help you identify which are the most cost-effective. A high CAC may signal that you need to optimize your ads or adjust your targeting, while a low CAC suggests you're getting a good return on your investment.

Evaluate Member Retention

While new member acquisition is important, retaining those members is just as crucial. Marketing isn't only about bringing people through the door—it's about keeping them engaged and loyal to your gym. That's why it's important to track your **member retention rate** as well.

Are the new members you're gaining through a particular campaign sticking around, or are they leaving after a month or two? This can provide insight into the effectiveness of your messaging and whether your gym is delivering on the promises made in your marketing. If your retention rate is low, it might be worth revisiting your onboarding process or member experience to ensure new members feel supported and motivated to stay.

Make Data-Driven Adjustments

Once you've gathered data on your marketing efforts, the real value comes from analyzing that information and using it to make informed decisions. Look for trends in your data. Are certain types of campaigns consistently performing better? Is there a particular audience segment that responds more positively to your messaging? These insights can guide your future marketing strategy.

If a campaign isn't performing as expected, don't be afraid to adjust it. This might mean refining your ad copy, changing your targeting parameters, or reallocating your budget to higher-performing channels. The key is to remain flexible and responsive to the data, rather than sticking rigidly to a plan that isn't working.

Set Clear Goals

Finally, measuring and analyzing your marketing success is easier when you have clear, defined goals. Whether you're aiming to increase member sign-ups by 20% or grow your social media following by a certain number, having specific objectives helps you gauge whether your efforts are on track. Regularly checking your progress against these goals ensures that you stay focused and can celebrate wins when you achieve them.

Measuring marketing success isn't just about looking at numbers—it's about understanding what's driving your gym's growth and making smart, data-informed decisions that keep you moving forward.

Chapter 6

Operational Excellence and Efficiency

Streamlining Gym Operations

Running a gym smoothly requires more than just great equipment and a dedicated staff. The day-to-day operations need to be efficient, organized, and responsive to the needs of both members and employees. Streamlining operations not only makes the gym more enjoyable for everyone but also saves time and reduces costs. Focusing on efficiency helps ensure your gym runs like a well-oiled machine, allowing you to focus more on growth and member satisfaction.

Optimized Gym Floor Plan. Source: technogym.com

Note:
"If you're looking for tools to design or optimize your gym's interior, check out <u>Technogym Interior Design Tool</u>, or scan the QR below. This platform helps you create customized layouts for an efficient, professional, and welcoming space."

Optimizing Scheduling

Effective scheduling is key to making sure both staff and gym resources are used wisely. This means creating a balanced timetable for group classes, personal training sessions, and maintenance tasks that don't disrupt members. A well-structured schedule ensures that classes are spaced out so equipment and space aren't overcrowded, and that trainers have enough time to give clients their full attention.

Using software to manage schedules can be a game-changer. It allows members to easily book classes or training sessions online, while also helping staff track their own availability. This eliminates confusion and ensures that no one is double-booked, making the whole process smoother for everyone involved.

Automating Administrative Tasks

One of the best ways to streamline gym operations is by automating repetitive administrative tasks. Tasks like membership sign-ups, payment processing, and sending out reminders for renewals or class bookings can all be handled by management software. Automating these processes reduces the chance of human error and frees up your staff to focus on providing great service rather than getting bogged down in paperwork.

Additionally, automation helps improve communication with your members. For example, automatic emails can remind them of upcoming classes, offer new membership deals, or even send out personalized fitness tips. This keeps your gym top of mind without requiring constant manual effort.

Efficient Inventory Management

Whether it's gym supplies, retail items, or even towels and cleaning products, staying on top of inventory is crucial to maintaining smooth operations. Running out of essential items during busy times can be frustrating for members and disrupt the flow of your gym. To avoid this, establish a system to track inventory levels in real-time.

Inventory management software can help you monitor stock levels, set up automatic reordering, and ensure you're not over- or under-stocked. Keeping supplies well-managed helps avoid unnecessary delays and ensures that members always have what they need for a successful workout.

Maintaining Equipment Regularly

Nothing throws off a gym's rhythm more than broken or malfunctioning equipment. To prevent disruptions, it's important to have a routine maintenance schedule in place. Regularly checking and servicing machines, weights, and other gym equipment not only keeps everything in working order but also extends the lifespan of your investments.

Establish a system where trainers or staff can quickly report any issues, and ensure that repairs are made promptly. This proactive approach minimizes downtime and keeps members happy since they won't have to wait for their favorite machines or worry about safety concerns.

Improving Member Feedback Systems

Listening to your members is one of the most effective ways to identify areas that need improvement. Setting up a system where members can easily provide feedback—whether it's through online surveys, suggestion boxes, or apps—allows you to quickly address any issues and refine your operations.

Responding to feedback not only helps resolve problems before they grow but also shows members that you value their input. This can build stronger relationships and encourage loyalty, as members feel heard and appreciated. Streamlining your feedback process ensures you stay responsive to your community's needs.

Simplifying Membership Management

Managing memberships is one of the most important operational tasks, but it doesn't have to be complicated. Simplifying this process can make a huge difference in how smoothly your gym runs. Use software that allows members to easily sign up, renew their memberships, or upgrade their plans online. This minimizes the back-and-forth communication and makes it easy for members to manage their accounts on their own time.

Offering flexible membership options, such as short-term passes or pay-as-you-go options, can also streamline operations by reducing the complexity of managing long-term contracts for every member. The easier you make it for people to sign up and stay with your gym, the smoother your operations will be.

By focusing on efficiency and utilizing technology where possible, you can streamline your gym's operations, freeing up time and resources to improve the overall experience for your members. A well-run gym not only feels better to be in but also builds a stronger, more loyal membership base.

Staff Training and Development

The success of your gym relies heavily on the quality and expertise of your staff. Whether it's front desk personnel, trainers, or support staff, each team member plays a crucial role in creating a positive experience for your members. Investing in staff training and development not only improves the service you provide but also helps build a loyal, motivated team that stays with your business long-term.

Creating a Culture of Continuous Learning

In the fitness industry, trends, techniques, and technologies are always evolving. To stay competitive and offer the best services to your members, it's essential to foster a culture of continuous learning within your team. This means encouraging staff to regularly update their knowledge and skills, whether through certifications, workshops, or in-house training sessions.

For personal trainers, this might involve keeping up with the latest research in exercise science or learning new workout modalities like functional training or recovery techniques. For front desk staff, it could mean training on the latest gym management software or improving customer service skills. When your staff feels empowered to grow and learn, they're more likely to stay engaged and provide a higher level of service.

Focusing on Customer Service Skills

While technical expertise is important, soft skills like communication and customer service can make or break a member's experience. Members often form a connection with your gym based on how they're treated, and friendly, helpful staff can be the deciding factor in whether someone sticks around or leaves for another facility.

Training your staff to engage with members in a positive, welcoming way should be a top priority. This includes teaching them how to handle inquiries, resolve complaints, and anticipate member needs. Role-playing different scenarios can be a useful way to practice these skills and prepare your team to handle a variety of situations with confidence.

Ongoing Personal Development for Trainers

For personal trainers, development should go beyond technical fitness knowledge. Great trainers are not only experts in their field, but they are also motivators, mentors, and even role models for many members. Helping your trainers develop skills in communication, goal-setting, and emotional intelligence can make them even more effective in their roles.

Regular performance evaluations and feedback sessions can help trainers identify areas for growth and improvement. Encourage them to set personal and professional goals, and provide the resources they need to achieve them. Whether it's additional training in nutrition or learning how to better engage with clients on social media, ongoing development ensures your trainers are equipped to meet the diverse needs of your members.

Team Building and Collaboration

Creating a strong team dynamic is essential for the overall success of your gym. Staff training shouldn't only focus on individual skills but also emphasize teamwork and collaboration. When staff members from different departments work well together, it enhances the overall member experience.

Regular team-building activities, staff meetings, and collaborative problem-solving sessions can help foster a sense of unity among your team. When everyone feels like they are working toward the same goal—providing the best experience for your members—it creates a more positive and efficient work environment.

Developing Leadership from Within

As your gym grows, you may need to promote staff into leadership or management positions. Identifying and developing potential leaders from within your current team can be a great way to ensure continuity and loyalty. Leadership development programs, mentorship opportunities, or providing additional responsibilities are all effective ways to nurture future leaders.

Encouraging staff to take ownership of their roles and develop leadership qualities not only benefits your gym but also helps staff feel valued and invested in their careers. This can lead to higher job satisfaction and lower turnover, which ultimately saves you time and resources in hiring and training new staff.

Investing in staff training and development pays off in countless ways, from improved member satisfaction to a more motivated, knowledgeable, and loyal team. When your staff feels equipped to succeed, it creates a better environment for everyone involved.

Utilizing Data for Continuous Improvement

Data is one of the most valuable tools you can use to improve your gym's operations and enhance the member experience. By gathering and analyzing data, you can make informed decisions that lead to better results. The key is knowing how to collect the right information and turn it into actionable insights that drive continuous improvement. When used correctly, data helps you identify trends, track performance, and find new opportunities to grow your gym business.

Tracking Member Behavior

One of the most important types of data to collect is information about how your members use your gym. This includes when they visit, which classes or equipment they prefer, and how often they attend. Tracking member behavior allows you to see patterns that can help you make decisions about staffing, scheduling, and even marketing.

For example, if you notice that certain classes are always full while others struggle to get sign-ups, you can adjust your schedule to offer more of what's popular. If you find that members are frequently using particular machines, you might consider adding more of those to your gym or upgrading your equipment to meet demand. Understanding how members interact with your gym gives you a clear view of what's working and where you can make improvements.

Improving Retention with Data

Retention is critical for long-term success, and data can help you keep track of how well you're retaining members. By analyzing data on when members join, how long they stay, and when they tend to leave, you can identify potential drop-off points. This allows you to intervene early and address issues before they result in cancellations.

For example, if you see that many members tend to cancel their memberships after three months, you can investigate why this is happening. Perhaps there's a lack of motivation or engagement at this point in their fitness journey. With this knowledge, you could introduce special programs or check-ins during that time to keep members engaged and motivated to stay.

Measuring Marketing Effectiveness

Data plays a big role in determining the success of your marketing efforts. By tracking which campaigns bring in the most new members and which channels (such as social media, email, or search ads) are driving the best results, you can optimize your marketing strategy. For instance, if you notice that a particular type of social media post consistently performs well, you can create more content in that style to attract new members.

Additionally, data can help you understand the lifetime value of a member. If certain promotions bring in members who stay longer and spend more, those are the types of campaigns you'll want to focus on in the future. Tracking this data ensures that your marketing dollars are being spent in the most effective way possible.

Enhancing the Member Experience

The member experience is at the heart of your gym's success, and data can provide valuable insights into how well you're meeting your members' needs. Regularly collecting feedback through surveys or online reviews helps you understand what members like about your gym and where they feel improvements could be made. By paying attention to patterns in the feedback, you can prioritize changes that will have the most impact.

For example, if several members mention that certain areas of the gym feel crowded or that the wait time for machines is too long, you can take steps to address these concerns. This might involve rearranging the layout of your gym, adding more equipment, or adjusting class sizes to better manage the flow of people. Listening to what your members are saying and backing it up with data ensures that the changes you make are both meaningful and effective.

Driving Operational Efficiency

Data can also help you streamline your gym's operations. By analyzing things like staffing levels, energy usage, and maintenance schedules, you can find ways to improve efficiency and reduce costs. For example, tracking which times of day are busiest can help you determine when to schedule more staff or trainers, ensuring that members get the attention they need without overstaffing during slower periods.

Similarly, tracking equipment usage can help you stay on top of maintenance needs. If you notice that certain machines are used more frequently, you can schedule more regular maintenance for them to prevent breakdowns and minimize downtime. This not only improves the member experience but also extends the life of your equipment.

Utilizing data in these ways helps you make informed decisions that continuously improve your gym's performance. It allows you to be proactive rather than reactive, solving problems before they affect your members and ultimately driving the success of your business.

Chapter 7

Financial Management for Sustainable Growth

Budgeting and Financial Planning

Running a successful gym requires more than just great equipment and dedicated members. One of the most crucial aspects of managing your business is ensuring that you have a solid financial foundation. Budgeting and financial planning are key to keeping your gym on track, helping you make informed decisions, and ensuring long-term success.

Understanding Your Revenue and Expenses

The first step in financial planning is having a clear understanding of your gym's revenue and expenses. Revenue isn't just about membership fees—although that's a large part of it. You also need to account for other income streams, such as personal training, group classes, merchandise sales, and additional services like massage therapy or nutrition consultations.

On the expense side, consider all your costs—both fixed and variable. Fixed expenses include things like rent, utilities, salaries, and equipment leases. These are the bills you have to pay each month, regardless of how many members you have. Variable expenses, on the other hand, can fluctuate. These might include marketing costs, supplies, and any commission-based wages for trainers. Having a clear picture of both types of expenses will help you better manage your finances.

Cash Flow Forecast for a Gym Business

USD

	Year 1	Year 2	Year 3
Net income	(125,936)	1,040,340	1,361,535
Plus depreciation	32,083	35,000	35,000
Less increase in inventory	(11,351)	(110,217)	(13,508)
Less increase in accounts receivable	-	-	-
Plus increase in accounts payable	9,330	90,589	11,102
Cash flow from operations	**(95,874)**	**1,055,712**	**1,394,130**
Less investment	(350,000)	-	-
Cash flow from operations & investment	**(445,874)**	**1,055,712**	**1,394,130**
Plus net new equity capital raised	470,000	-	-
Less dividends paid	-	-	-
Plus net new long-term debt	-	-	-
Plus net new bank borrowings	-	-	-
Cash flow from ops, invest & financing	**24,126**	**1,055,712**	**1,394,130**
Beginning cash balance	-	24,126	1,079,838
Ending cash balance	24,126	1,079,838	2,473,968

Cash Flow Projection for a Gym Business. Source: businessandplans.com

Creating a Realistic Budget

Once you have a handle on your income and expenses, the next step is creating a realistic budget. Your budget serves as a roadmap for how you will allocate your resources over time. Start by projecting your revenue based on current membership numbers and other income streams. Be conservative in your estimates to avoid overestimating your cash flow.

Next, outline all of your necessary expenses, making sure to prioritize essential costs like rent, payroll, and utilities. Then, allocate funds for areas that will help grow your business, such as marketing and staff development. It's also important to set aside a portion of your budget for unexpected costs or emergencies, like equipment repairs or a sudden drop in membership.

Having a budget in place helps ensure that you're not overspending and gives you a clear sense of where your money is going each month.

Cash Flow Management

Cash flow is the movement of money in and out of your business, and managing it effectively is critical to your gym's survival. Even if you're profitable on paper, cash flow issues can arise if your expenses come due before your revenue is collected. To avoid this, monitor your cash flow regularly to ensure you always have enough liquidity to cover your costs.

One way to improve cash flow is to offer incentives for members to pay annually instead of monthly, bringing in larger sums of money upfront. Additionally, keeping a close eye on your accounts receivable—making sure payments are collected on time—can help prevent cash flow shortages.

Planning for Growth

Financial planning isn't just about managing your current situation—it's about planning for the future. As your gym grows, you may want to expand by opening new locations, adding more services, or upgrading your facilities. These goals require careful financial planning to ensure they're sustainable.

When planning for growth, consider both the initial costs and the ongoing expenses. For example, opening a second location involves not just the cost of leasing and outfitting a new space but also additional salaries, utilities, and marketing efforts. By carefully forecasting these costs and comparing them to your projected revenue, you can determine whether a growth opportunity is financially feasible.

It's also helpful to create financial milestones, such as reaching a certain number of members or increasing your revenue by a set percentage. These goals will guide your financial decisions and help you track your progress over time.

Reviewing and Adjusting Your Financial Plan

No financial plan is set in stone. It's important to regularly review your budget and financial projections to ensure they align with your gym's actual performance. If your revenue is higher than expected, you may have room to reinvest in your business or expand your marketing efforts. If it's lower, you'll need to adjust your expenses or find ways to increase income.

Regular financial reviews also allow you to spot potential issues before they become serious problems. By staying proactive with your budgeting and financial planning, you can keep your gym on solid financial footing and set yourself up for long-term success.

Managing Cash Flow

Effective cash flow management is essential for running a successful gym. Cash flow represents the money moving in and out of your business, and keeping a steady balance between the two ensures that your gym operates smoothly. If you don't have enough cash on hand to cover expenses, even a profitable gym can run into financial trouble. Understanding how to manage cash flow will help you anticipate financial needs, avoid shortfalls, and keep your business running efficiently.

Understanding Your Cash Flow Cycle

The first step in managing cash flow is understanding your gym's cash flow cycle. This refers to the timing of when money comes into your business (income) and when it goes out (expenses). For many gyms, income primarily comes from membership fees, class fees, personal training, and retail sales. Expenses include rent, utilities, equipment maintenance, staff salaries, and other operational costs.

It's important to recognize that income and expenses don't always align perfectly. For example, membership fees might be collected at the beginning of the month, while expenses like rent and utilities are due throughout the month. Understanding this cycle helps you plan ahead and ensure that you have enough cash available when you need it.

Monitoring Cash Flow Regularly

To keep a close eye on your gym's financial health, it's important to monitor your cash flow regularly. This involves tracking how much money is coming in and going out over specific periods, such as weekly or monthly. Regular monitoring helps you spot potential cash flow issues before they become serious problems.

By reviewing cash flow statements, you can identify patterns and anticipate periods when you might need extra cash on hand. For instance, if you notice that your gym tends to have lower cash flow during certain months due to seasonal fluctuations, you can plan accordingly and make adjustments to avoid a shortfall.

Managing Income Timing

One effective way to improve cash flow is by adjusting how and when you collect income. For example, offering incentives for members to pay for longer-term memberships upfront can give you more cash in hand early on. Encouraging annual or six-month memberships, instead of relying solely on month-to-month payments, can provide a more consistent and predictable cash flow.

Additionally, having clear and efficient billing practices ensures that payments are collected on time. If your gym offers personal training or additional services, implementing automated payment systems can reduce late or missed payments and keep cash flow steady.

Controlling Expenses

Managing cash flow isn't just about increasing income; it's also about controlling expenses. While some costs, like rent and utilities, are fixed, other operational expenses may be more flexible. Regularly reviewing your expenses and finding ways to reduce unnecessary spending can help improve your cash flow.

For example, you can negotiate better rates with suppliers, switch to energy-efficient lighting to reduce utility bills, or consider leasing equipment instead of purchasing it outright. Even small savings can add up and make a big difference in maintaining a healthy cash flow.

Building a Cash Reserve

One of the best ways to protect your gym from cash flow issues is by building a cash reserve. A cash reserve acts as a financial cushion, providing funds that you can rely on during slower months or unexpected expenses. Setting aside a portion of your income each month into this reserve can help you cover shortfalls without having to rely on loans or credit.

Having a cash reserve gives you peace of mind and flexibility, allowing you to handle any financial surprises that come your way. Whether it's a sudden equipment repair or a seasonal dip in membership, a cash reserve ensures that your gym can weather the storm without disrupting daily operations.

Planning for Growth

As your gym grows, managing cash flow becomes even more critical. Whether you're expanding your space, adding new services, or hiring more staff, each of these initiatives requires careful financial planning. Understanding how these changes will impact your cash flow allows you to make informed decisions and avoid overstretching your resources.

Planning for growth means balancing short-term needs with long-term investments. While it can be tempting to invest in new equipment or services to attract more members, it's important to ensure that you have the cash flow to support these expenses without straining your business. Managing cash flow effectively helps you grow sustainably and keeps your gym on solid financial ground.

Managing cash flow is about staying proactive and making sure that your gym always has enough cash available to meet its financial obligations. By understanding your cash flow cycle, regularly monitoring finances, controlling expenses, and building a cash reserve, you set your business up for long-term success.

Investment and Expansion Strategies

Once your gym is running smoothly and generating steady revenue, it's natural to start thinking about ways to grow. Investing in the right areas and planning for expansion can significantly increase your business's profitability and help you reach new markets. However, careful planning is key to ensuring that your investment leads to sustainable growth rather than overextending your resources.

Evaluating When to Expand

The decision to expand your gym should be based on both your financial stability and member demand. Before taking any major steps, it's important to assess your current gym's performance. Are you consistently meeting or exceeding membership goals? Is your facility operating at or near capacity? If you're regularly experiencing high member engagement and demand for more services, it may be a sign that your business is ready to expand.

It's also crucial to evaluate your financial position. Expansion often requires a significant upfront investment, whether you're adding new equipment, expanding your space, or opening a second location. Make sure your gym has enough cash flow to support these expenses without compromising your current operations. Understanding your finances clearly will help you make smarter investment decisions.

Investing in Facility Upgrades

One of the most common ways to invest in your gym is by upgrading your current facilities. This can include adding new, state-of-the-art equipment, expanding your workout spaces, or updating locker rooms and other amenities. These types of improvements can make your gym more appealing to both current and potential members, helping you attract a broader audience.

Before making any upgrades, consider what your members value most. Conduct surveys or speak directly with members to understand their preferences. For instance, if members often complain about overcrowded classes or limited equipment availability, investing in additional machines or expanding class areas could have a direct impact on member satisfaction and retention.

Introducing New Services

Another way to grow your gym is by introducing new services that complement your existing offerings. This can range from adding personal training and specialized group classes to offering wellness programs like nutrition counseling, massage therapy, or recovery services. New services not only provide more value to your members but also create additional revenue streams for your business.

When adding new services, think about what will resonate with your target audience. For example, if you cater to busy professionals, consider offering express fitness classes or virtual training sessions that fit into their schedules. If your gym attracts a more holistic wellness crowd, services like yoga, mindfulness training, or health coaching might be more effective. By diversifying your offerings, you can appeal to a wider range of members while deepening the relationship with your existing clientele.

Expanding to a New Location

Opening a second (or third) location is a major step in expanding your gym business. It offers the opportunity to reach entirely new markets and increase your overall membership base.

However, expanding to a new location requires careful planning and significant investment.

The first step is to conduct thorough market research to identify areas with high demand for fitness services but limited competition. Look for growing neighborhoods or underserved communities where your gym can fill a gap in the market. Understanding the demographics and preferences of the local population is essential for choosing the right location and tailoring your services to meet their needs.

Next, consider the operational challenges of managing multiple locations. Each new gym will require its own staff, equipment, and marketing strategy. It's important to ensure that your management team is prepared to handle the complexities of running a multi-location business. Implementing standardized processes across all locations can help maintain consistency and ensure that each gym operates efficiently.

Franchising as a Growth Strategy

If you've built a successful and scalable gym model, franchising could be an attractive option for expansion. Franchising allows you to grow your brand without taking on all the risks and responsibilities of opening and managing new locations yourself. Instead, you partner with franchisees who invest their own capital to open new gyms under your brand.

Franchising requires a strong, well-defined business model that can be easily replicated across different locations. You'll need to provide franchisees with clear guidelines, training, and support to ensure that each new gym maintains the same level of quality and service as your original location. While franchising can be a profitable way to expand, it's important to thoroughly research and plan for the legal and operational complexities involved.

Partnering with Local Businesses

Another expansion strategy is to form partnerships with local businesses. This can include creating corporate wellness programs, where you offer discounted memberships or tailored fitness services to employees of nearby companies. Corporate partnerships provide a steady stream of clients and increase your visibility within the community.

You can also collaborate with businesses that complement your gym's offerings, such as nutritionists, physical therapists, or wellness centers. These partnerships allow you to offer a more comprehensive wellness experience to your members while generating referrals from your partners. Building strong relationships with local businesses can enhance your gym's reputation and help attract new members from different sources.

Expanding your gym takes time, careful planning, and smart investment. Whether you're upgrading your facilities, launching new services, or opening new locations, a strategic approach ensures that each step you take leads to sustainable growth and greater success for your business.

Conclusion

Building and running a successful gym is about much more than just offering a place for people to work out. Throughout this book, we've explored the key strategies for maximizing revenue and member retention—two of the most crucial aspects of creating a sustainable gym business. From understanding your market and creating a compelling value proposition to diversifying your revenue streams and fostering a strong community, each piece of the puzzle plays an important role in your gym's growth.

At the core of every successful gym is the ability to connect with members on a deeper level. Personalized training, exceptional customer service, and a supportive environment all contribute to making your gym more than just a fitness facility. When members feel valued, understood, and part of a community, they stay longer, and that loyalty drives your gym's long-term success.

In an ever-changing market, adaptability is key. Whether it's embracing new fitness trends, incorporating the latest technologies, or evolving your services to meet shifting demands, the ability to stay flexible ensures that your gym remains relevant and continues to thrive. Remember that innovation isn't just about keeping up with trends; it's about truly understanding your members' needs and providing solutions that help them succeed in their fitness journey.

This book is not just a guide—it's a blueprint for turning your gym into a thriving business that stands out in a crowded market. The success formula outlined here is meant to be practical and actionable, giving you the tools to take your gym to the next level. As you move forward, the key is to keep learning, adapting, and staying committed to delivering the best possible experience for your members.

The journey to building a successful gym business is both challenging and rewarding. By applying the insights and strategies from this book, you're well on your way to creating a space where members not only achieve their fitness goals but also feel part of something bigger. Now is the time to put these ideas into action, refine your approach, and build a gym that continues to grow and succeed in the years to come.

Dear Reader,

I hope you found the book insightful and valuable.

Your feedback is invaluable to me. If you enjoyed reading this book, I would appreciate it if you could take a moment to leave a review on the reading apps and platforms.

Thank you for your support, and I wish you all the best.

Kind regards,
Ghazwan

About the Author

Ghazwan is a passionate entrepreneur and business strategist dedicated to helping individuals and organizations achieve their full potential with a deep understanding of modern businesses' challenges and opportunities.

With a Master's degree in Computer and Systems Sciences from Stockholm University, specializing in eService design, requirement engineering, and business process management, he is equipped to innovate cutting-edge solutions.

He believes in the power of collaboration and lifelong learning, and his mission is to empower people to reach their goals and positively impact the world.

www.ingramcontent.com/pod-product-compliance
Lightning Source LLC
Chambersburg PA
CBHW071653240526
45469CB00021B/2279